BE CREATIVE

Bedroom Makeover

Anna Claybourne

W
FRANKLIN WATTS
LONDON • SYDNEY

First published in 2012 by
Franklin Watts
338 Euston Road
London NW1 3BH

Franklin Watts Australia
Level 17/207 Kent Street
Sydney NSW 2000

Copyright © Franklin Watts 2012

Produced for Franklin Watts by

White-Thomson Publishing
+44 (0)843 208 7460
www.wtpub.co.uk

Author: **Anna Claybourne**
Project manager: **Rachel Minay**
Creative director: **Simon Balley**
Design: **Balley Design Limited**
Designer/Illustrator: **Andrew Li**

The author has asserted her moral rights.

A CIP catalogue record for this book is available from the British Library.

ISBN: 978 1 4451 0552 9

Dewey Classification: 747.7'7

Picture Credits
aboikis 23, AKaiser 24/25, Alaettin YILDIRIM 4–5/16–17, Alena Ozerova 11, Ana Vasileva
4/12/13, Andrea Slatter 29, Aprilphoto 2/26/30, AVAVA 5, Baloncici 12/13, Crystal Kirk 18,
Dmitry Melnikov 2/4/30–31/32, Ed Phillips 2/4/20/21/30, Elena Elisseeva 25, Elena
Schweitzer 12/14/18/21, ericlefrancais 26, J. Broadwater 13, Jiri Hera 13/14/32, karam Miri
front cover/2/3/5/10/11/13/18/30–31, Karkas 4/13, Kayros Studio "Be Happy!" 13, Kimberly
Hall 3/5/8/14/16/18/20/31/32, Madlen 27/28, marymary 3/4/5/6/12/13/22/23/30/31, Masterov
Egor 28, Monkey Business Images front cover/19/23, Morozova Oxana 19, Nataliia
Melnychuk 18, NatesPics 21, Nattika 3/4/10/17, newyear2008 14/15, Olga K front
cover/5/8/9/16/17, qingqing 7, R. Cherubin 28/29, Ramon Berk 29, Razvy 13, Roman
Peregontsev front cover/5/8/9/16/17, ronstik 22, Solar 23, Steve Cukrov 3/27/31/32/back
cover, STILLFX 27, trekandshoot 29, Tupungato 29, vnlit 29, wacpan 27.

Every attempt has been made to clear copyright. Should there be any inadvertent omissions,
please apply to the publisher for rectification.

Note: Every effort has been made by the Publishers to ensure that the websites on page 30 of
this book are suitable for children and that they contain no inappropriate or offensive material.
However, because of the nature of the Internet, it is impossible to guarantee that the contents
of these sites will not be altered. We strongly advise that Internet access is supervised by a
responsible adult.

Printed in China.

Franklin Watts is a division of Hachette Children's Books, an Hachette UK Company.
www.hachette.co.uk

Contents

Words in **bold** are in the glossary on page 31.

Creative thinking

It's time to get creative! More and more people are making, crafting and designing their own stuff. It's satisfying and fun to do, and it means that you can have things that no one else has. It saves you money too! If you really enjoy it, you could even end up designing or making things for a living.

Get the gear!

The projects in this book mostly use sewing and craft materials such as card, glue, felt, fabric, thread, pins, needles, ribbons and buttons. You may have a lot of these at home anyway. If not, there's an equipment guide on page 30 to show you where you can find them.

A room of your own

Your bedroom is your own place, where you can chill out with friends, read, chat or spend time on hobbies. Use the projects in this book to stamp your own style on your space – as well as making it more cosy and comfy.

Safety

Remember to keep strings, cords and sharp things like pins, needles and scissors away from small children.

Tip!
You don't have to follow all the projects exactly. If you like, you can use the ideas and methods in this book to come up with your own original creations.

Reuse and recycle

Crafting can help to save the planet! For a lot of the projects in this book you can reuse old clothes, fabrics, card and other things, instead of buying new stuff that uses up the **Earth's resources** or sending old stuff into **landfill**.

Tip!
If you have a sewing machine and know how it works, you can use it for some of the projects in this book.

5

Little birds

These cute birds are easy to make. Hang them from your window frame, wall or bed.

Get the gear!

- Tracing paper and pencil
- 2 pieces of felt fabric, about 12cm square
- Scissors, pins and needles
- Colourful strong thread or **embroidery** thread
- Tape measure or ruler
- About 10cm of thin ribbon or wool
- Handful of soft toy stuffing (from a craft shop) – or you can use bundled-up knitting wool
- 2 buttons or beads for eyes

1 Trace this bird shape onto tracing paper, and cut it out.

2 Lay your two pieces of felt one on top of the other, and pin the paper shape on top. Then cut around the shape, through both layers of felt. Take off the pins and paper.

3 Make your piece of ribbon or wool into a loop and put it between the felt pieces, as shown. Pin the two pieces together, leaving enough space to sew around the edge of the bird.

4 Thread your needle and tie a knot in the long end. Sew around the edge of the bird, using **running stitch** (see box below). Sew about 0.5cm in from the edge. Make sure you also sew through the ribbon or wool to hold it in place.

5 When you're nearly all the way around, stop sewing, leaving a gap about 4cm wide. Remove the pins. Poke in some toy stuffing or wool. Finish sewing along the gap, knot the thread and snip off.

6 Finish off by sewing on two small buttons or beads for eyes (see box on page 13).

How to do running stitch

Running stitch is a very simple stitch where you simply sew in and out of the fabric in a straight line. It is most useful for sewing thick fabrics, to **gather** fabrics or to make a decorative stitch.

Tip!
If you're hanging your bird up high, or need to put in a hook or nail to hang it from, ask an adult to help.

Bedroom bunting

In the past, **bunting** was just used for fairs and street parties. But now indoor bunting is a big trend. String it up to decorate your room – you can have it any colour or pattern you like.

Get the gear!

- 1 big piece of fabric (felt or fleece is recommended) or several smaller pieces of different colours or patterns
- About 3–5m of ribbon or **fabric tape** about 2cm wide
- Tape measure and scissors
- Pins, needles and thread

1 Bunting flags can be large or small, but a good size is about 10cm wide at the base and 15cm long. To make a flag, measure and cut out a triangle-shaped piece of fabric.

10cm

15cm

Tip!
Cut triangles like this to avoid wasting any fabric.

2 For each metre of ribbon or tape you will need about 4 flags. So for 3m of ribbon or tape, you will need 12 flags.

1m

Safety

Keep bunting away from young children and babies. Ask an adult to help you hang it up safely so that it can't fall down.

3 Lay your ribbon or tape flat, and arrange the flags along it, one every 25cm.

25cm

4 Fold the ribbon or tape over so it covers the wide end of each triangle, and pin in place.

5 Then sew along the pinned line using **backstitch** (see box below), removing the pins as you go.

How to do backstitch

1 Push the needle tip in and out of the fabric, making a small stitch.

2 Go back to where the thread disappears into the fabric and push the needle in.

3 Do another stitch, coming out a bit further along.

4 Do the same with each stitch, going back to fill in the space left by the stitch before.

Tip!
Use backstitch when you need a strong seam or **hem**.

1

2

3

4

Cushion cover

Cushions make your room feel cosy, friendly and comfy. Make loads and you can relax in a big pile of them! Cotton, velvet, fake fur or fleece fabric make good cushion covers.

Get the gear

- **Cushion inner** or an old cushion to re-cover. 45cm square is a good size, but it can be any size.
- Fabric
- Scissors and tape measure
- Pins, needles and thread
- About 30cm of ribbon if you want a removable cover

1

Measure your cushion and cut a piece of fabric that's twice as wide (e.g. 45cm x 2 = 90cm) and as long (45cm), plus an extra 3cm all around.

3cm

45cm

45cm

2

Fold the fabric in half 'right sides together', which means that the patterned or 'best' sides are face to face. Then pin the fabric together along the top and bottom, 3cm in from the edge.

3

Now backstitch (see page 9) along the pinned line on each side of the cushion, removing the pins as you go. At the end of each side, knot the thread and snip off.

4 Fold the **raw edge** of the opening over twice to make a hem (neat edge). Pin along it, then sew all the way around using backstitch. Remove the pins. Remember – you don't want to sew it shut because the cushion needs to go inside!

Tip!
Ironing the hem flat will give a sharper edge and make it easier to sew. You should ask an adult to help you.

5 Turn the cover the right way out. If you want a removable cover, sew two 15cm pieces of ribbon to the opening using backstitch, so that you can tie the cover closed once the cushion is inside. If not, just insert the cushion and then sew the opening up using **overstitch** (see box below).

How to do overstitch

1 Thread your needle and knot the long end of the thread.

2 Push the needle tip through both fabrics and pull towards you over the top, making a stitch that pulls the two edges together.

3 Move the needle along slightly and do the same again. Keep stitching like this all the way along, then knot the thread and snip off.

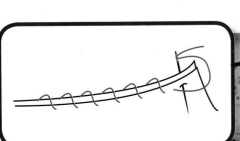

Decorated cushion

Once you can make a basic cushion cover, get creative with different decorative designs. These work best on plain, flat fabrics.

Get the gear!

- Cushion inner or old cushion, and fabric to cover it, as on page 10
- About 30cm of ribbon
- Scissors and tape measure
- Pins, needles and thread
- Buttons, beads, wool or embroidery thread, scraps of felt or fleece fabric

Tip!
Make a fluffy fake fur cushion into a bedroom monster by sewing on toy eyes (you can buy them at craft shops).

1 Spread out your fabric. Choose which half will be the top, and use pins to mark where you want your design. It's easiest to add the design before putting the cover on the cushion. Three things to try are on page 13.

2 When you have added the design, sew the cushion cover together as on pages 10–11.

Line art

Use bright-coloured wool or embroidery thread and a large needle. Knot the thread, and sew in from the back of the fabric. Then stitch a line of backstitch (see page 9) in the shape of a picture or pattern. You could even spell out words.

Buttons and beads

Sew on small buttons or beads (see box below) to make a pattern, or a shape such as a flower or face.

Appliqué

Appliqué means 'applying' a fabric picture to something. Cut out a felt or fleece shape, such as a heart or animal. Pin it onto your cushion fabric, then sew it on using backstitch. You can sew beads or buttons on top too.

Sewing on beads and buttons

Thread a needle and knot the end of the thread. Sew through from the back or inside of the fabric, and push the needle through the holes in the button or bead. Then sew through to the back again. Repeat several times before knotting at the back.

Panel curtain

A panel curtain is a flat, **sheer** curtain that hangs straight down over your window (inside the main curtains). It lets in light, but keeps your room private.

Get the gear!

- Large piece of light, non-stretchy fabric, such as cotton voile, silk or muslin, a bit bigger than your window
- Tape measure and scissors
- Pins, needles and thread
- Ribbon, fabric tape or string

1 First, measure the space you want your curtain to cover. This is probably slightly bigger than your window pane, so as to overlap the window frame. For the curtain, you need a piece of fabric this size, plus about 5cm all round.

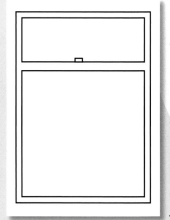

2 Lay the fabric flat, with the patterned or 'right' side down. Fold the edge in 2.5cm; then fold over again to make a hem. It's easiest to do the long sides first, then the ends, so that the corners are folded in neatly. Pin the hem in place all round the edge.

hem

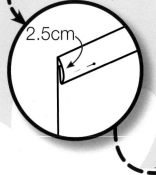

2.5cm

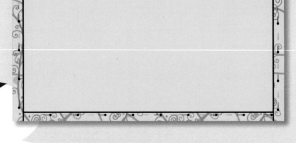

3 Thread your needle and sew along the hem using backstitch (see page 9) or a sewing machine if you have one. Take out the pins as you go.

4 Use backstitch or overstitch (sees pages 9 and 11) to attach two loops of ribbon, fabric tape or string to the two top corners of the curtain.

5 Ask an adult to help you put two small hooks or nails into the window frame above the glass; then you can hang the curtain up by the loops.

Tip!
Make sure the length of the loops and the positioning of the hooks match up, so that your curtain hangs in the right place.

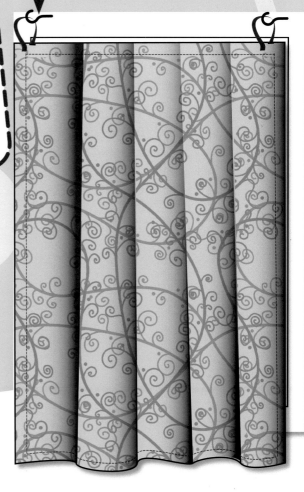

Handy pocket

This handy pocket is a bit like a shelf, but you can sew it! Use it to hang a book by your bed, pencils by your desk, or a remote control wherever you need it.

Get the gear!

- Quite strong, firm fabric such as thick cotton or canvas. For a book holder, use a piece about 50cm square.
- About 20cm of ribbon or fabric tape
- Scissors and ruler
- Pins, needles and thread

1 For a pocket to hold a normal-sized book, cut four pieces of fabric in two sizes, like this.

22cm
22cm
18cm
18cm

2 Take the two larger pieces and put them 'right sides together'. Pin them together all around the edge.

3 Sew the fabric pieces together, about 2cm in from the edge, using backstitch (see page 9). Leave a gap at one end about 10cm wide. Remove the pins.

10cm gap

4

Turn the sewn piece the right way out, pin the gap closed, and sew along it using backstitch. This is the back piece of the pocket.

Tip!
When turning right way out, use a ruler to push out the corners so they're nice and neat.

5

Do exactly the same thing with the smaller two pieces to make the front part of the pocket.

6

Now lay the front piece of the pocket on top of the back piece and pin it in place. Sew around the two sides and the bottom using backstitch.

7

Finally, sew two 10cm lengths of ribbon or tape to the top corners to make hanging loops. Ask an adult to help you put up hooks or nails so you can hang your pocket wherever you want it.

Tip!
If you like, sew on buttons, beads, ribbons or **sequins** as decoration.

Big bed throw

Transform your boring bed! All you need is a colourful, soft, snuggly or funkily patterned throw.

Get the gear!

- Big piece of fabric, at least 140cm x 160cm
- Ribbon (5cm wide or more), enough to go around your piece of fabric, plus 50cm
- Scissors
- Pins
- Needle and thread, or a sewing machine

1

Spread out your fabric. Fold the ribbon in half lengthways and start wrapping it around the edge of the fabric, pinning it in place as you go. Make sure the ribbon is folded neatly in half and the pins go through both sides of it.

2

At the corners, fold the ribbon over itself as you go round the corner, like this.

Tip!
Look for warm, cosy fabric, such as velvet, fleece or fake fur with a fab animal print!

ribbon tucked in

When you get back to where you started, trim the ribbon to the right length plus about 6cm. Fold the raw end of the ribbon inwards and pin it in place, overlapping the other end.

3

4

Finally, sew the fabric and ribbon together, close to the edge of the ribbon, removing the pins as you go. If you have a sewing machine, you can do this quickly, or do it by hand using backstitch (see page 9) or overstitch (see page 11). Make sure you go through both sides of the ribbon in each stitch.

Patchwork projects

Patchwork means sewing together bits of fabric to make a big, flat pattern. It's brilliant for using up fabric scraps and old clothes, and it looks amazing.

Get the gear

- Selection of different fabrics
- Sewing pins, needles and thread
- Scissors and a tape measure or ruler

1
You need lots of different fabrics for your patches. A good patch size to start with is 6cm square. Cut your fabric into 8cm squares (this will allow for sewing the edges together).

8cm

8cm

2
To sew two squares together, lay them on top of each other 'right sides together', and pin them together along one side. Then backstitch (see page 9) along that side, about 1cm from the edge. Remove the pins.

3
Open out the squares, and pin and sew a new square to one of them, like this.

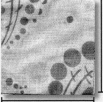

Tip!
Patchwork can be made up of any colour combination you like – shades of one colour, bright colours, pastels, or random bits and bobs. Or you can use the patches to create a design of stripes or shapes as you go.

4 Keep adding more in the same way, until you have a strip of five or ten squares (or any number you like).

5 Repeat until you have several strips. If possible, iron them (with an adult to help you), or just smooth them out flat.

6 To sew two strips together, lay them down 'right sides together', neatly lined up, and pin and backstitch along 1cm from the edge. Keep adding more strips in the same way – and you'll end up with your whole patchwork panel.

Tip!
You can use patchwork to make cushions, bedcovers or other projects in this book – or even for clothes!
If you really enjoy patchwork, experiment with patches of different sizes and shapes. You can use rectangles, triangles or hexagons.

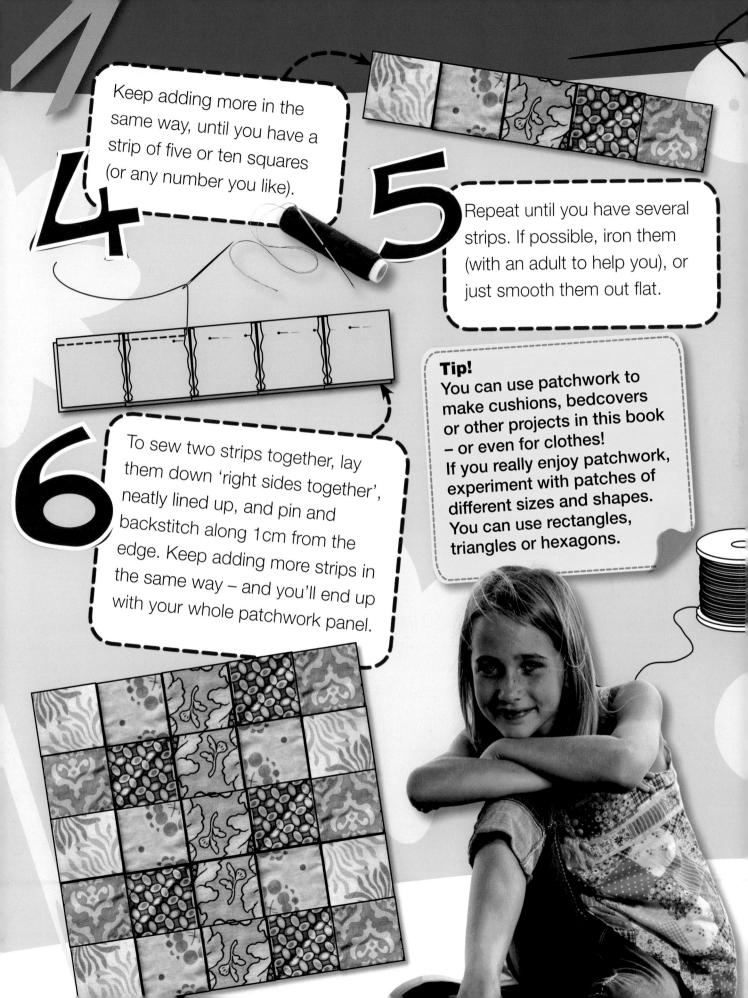

Photo frame

Put photos of family, friends or pets in your room, and give them their own funky frames.

Get the gear!

- Thick card, a few cm larger than the photo you want to frame
- Ruler, pencil and sticky tape
- Craft knife or sharp scissors
- Paper scraps, PVA glue and a brush, buttons, sequins, ribbons, stickers or glitter

1 First, draw a frame in the middle of your card. This can be a basic square or rectangle, or other shapes, but the inside of the frame needs to be slightly smaller than your photo. Carefully cut out the frame, using a craft knife. Ask an adult to help you.

2 To decorate the frame, try these ideas:

Decoupage

Decoupage means gluing things onto paper to make a smooth, colourful covering. Use bits of torn-up tissue paper, old wrapping paper, magazine pictures or old calendars. Paint PVA glue onto the frame, stick down a piece of paper, and cover it with more glue. Keep going, overlapping the pieces until the frame is covered. Leave to dry.

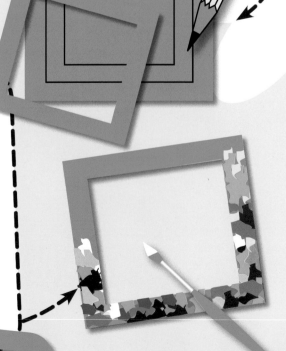

Collage

Stick ribbons, buttons, sequins or whatever you like onto your frame to decorate it. For example, you could cover it all over with little multicoloured buttons. Or wrap ribbon all the way around it and glue it in place at the back.

Tip!
If you are going to use collage but not cover the entire frame, you might want to start with coloured or sparkly card. Or you could stick colourful or interesting paper to your frame first.

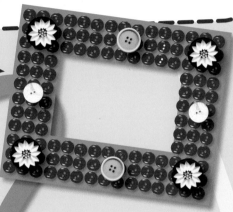

Fake it

Search for a photo of an old-fashioned, carved picture frame on the Internet, and print it out. Cut your card frame to the same size and glue the printed frame to it. Your fancy frame will make your photos look like works of fine art!

3 To attach the photo, put the frame face down, with your photo face down on top, making sure it overlaps the hole in the middle. Sticky tape the back of the photo to the frame.

Tip!
To make a cardboard stand for your photo, just cut a strip of card, fold it and tape it to the back of the frame.

Writing on the wall

Make a name sign to put on your door or decorate your wall.

Get the gear!

- Ready-made craft letters from a craft shop, or thick card for making your own
- Pencil
- Craft knife or sharp scissors
- Paper scraps, PVA glue and brush, paint or felt tips, sequins, glitter, stick-on googly eyes

1 To make your own letters, use quite thick, white or light-coloured card. Draw your letters onto the card, making them quite large (about 8cm high or bigger). If you're not sure what style and shape to make them, look in books and magazines for letter shapes to copy.

2 Cut out your letters carefully, using scissors or a craft knife (ask an adult to help).

3 Now decorate your letters! Look at the next page for some ideas.

Colours and patterns

Use paints or felt tips to cover your letters with colours, stripes, spots, animal markings, or whatever you like. You can stick on googly eyes, sequins or glitter too.

Decoupage

Cover your letters with paper scraps and PVA glue, using the decoupage method shown on page 22.

Font fun

Use a computer program such as Word to write big letters in interesting **fonts** and colours on the computer screen. Print them out, stick them onto the card and carefully cut them out.

When your letters are finished, pin or tack them to your bedroom door or onto a wall (check with an adult first) to spell out your name or any words you like.

Wall stencils

Jazz up your bedroom walls with patterns or pictures, using special decorating **stencils**. You can buy them, but it's more fun to make your own. (Check with a parent or carer before decorating your bedroom walls, though!)

Get the gear!

- Thin card
- Pencil
- Sharp scissors or a craft knife
- Removable sticky tape or masking tape
- Leftover emulsion wall paint or **acrylic paint**. Metallic paint would work well.
- Small decorating paintbrush or large art paintbrush
- Old clothes and newspapers

1 Draw your stencil designs onto card. They should be simple outline shapes, such as stars and moons, simple animals, hearts, arrows or leaves.

2 Carefully cut out the shapes, leaving the outline with a neat edge. This is easiest with a craft knife, resting on thick card such as the back of a pad of paper (ask an adult to help).

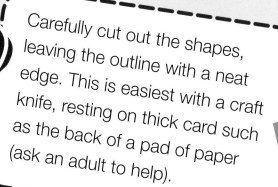

3

For the painting part, lay down plenty of old newspaper near the wall, and wear old clothes. Position each stencil on the wall where you want it, and attach with removable sticky tape.

Get a little paint on your brush and dab or wipe it to get rid of drips. Paint carefully inwards, over the edge of the stencil towards the middle of the design.

4

5

Leave until dry; then very carefully remove the stencil.

Recycled waste paper basket

Every bedroom needs a waste paper basket – and this one is made from recycled waste paper!

- Lots of old newspapers
- PVA glue or sticky tape
- Scissors

1 First make the strips your basket will be made from. Take a sheet of newspaper and fold it over and over to make a flat strip about 3cm wide and 60cm long. Use glue or sticky tape to hold it in place.

2 Now to make your basket. Take six strips and lie them down together. Take another strip, and weave it over and under the six strips, so it ends up in the middle, like this.

3 Take the next strip, and do the same, but go under the strips you went over before, and over the strips you went under before, like this.

4 Keep weaving until all six strips are in place like this. Then fold the strips up at the sides to make a box shape.

Tip! If your strips aren't long enough to go round, glue two together, end to end.

5 Weave a new strip all around the bottom of the basket. Stick it together at the ends to hold it in place.

6 Do the same with more strips to build up the sides of the basket. When you get to about 6cm from the top, fold the ends down inside the basket and stick them in place to make a neat edge.

Tip! Magazines or old wrapping paper make a really colourful version!

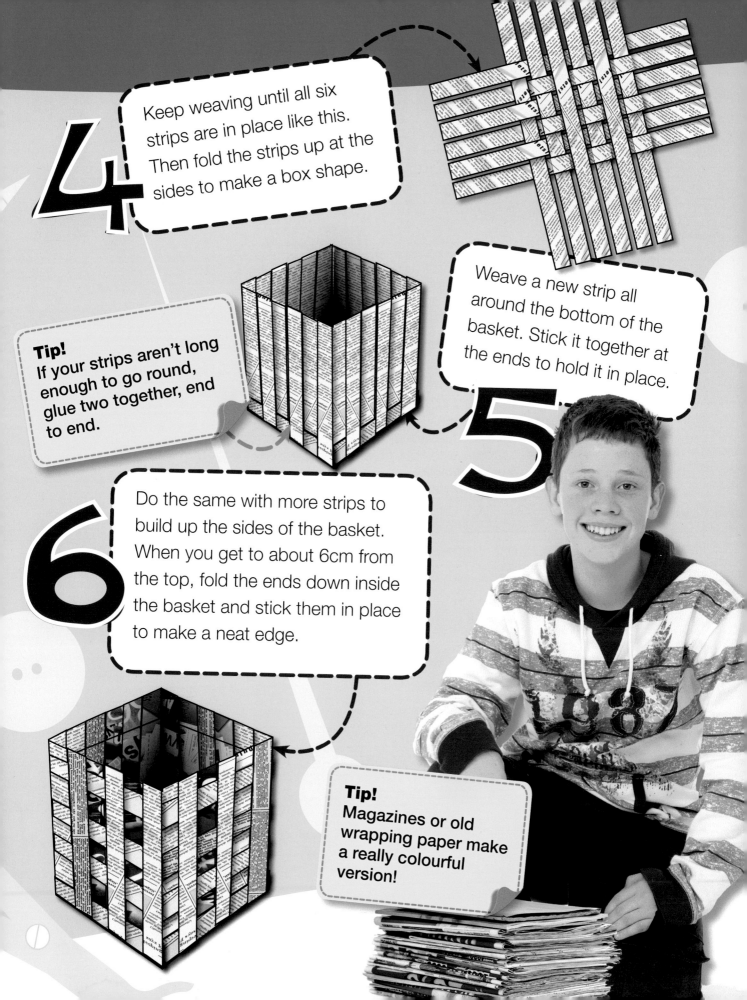

Equipment tips

Here's a quick guide to finding the things you need for your bedroom makeover projects.

Buttons and beads
Find these at sewing shops, craft shops, department stores and special bead shops. You can also check charity shops, jumble sales, and reuse buttons and beads from old clothes and jewellery.

Card
Stationery shops and art shops usually have several types of card. You can also reuse card from packaging for some projects.

Craft knife
You can get a good, easy-to-use craft knife at an art shop, craft shop or stationer's. Ask an adult to help you use it.

Craft letters
Some craft shops sell large wooden or cardboard letters.

Cushion inners
IKEA® and other home stores often have these.

Embroidery thread
This is often sold in sewing and craft shops or knitting shops, and comes in hundreds of colours. Look for good quality, cotton thread, such as Anchor, which is easy to use and washable.

Fabric
Fabric shops, craft shops and some department stores sell new fabrics by the metre. Check bargain buckets for cheaper **remnants**. IKEA® is great for cheap, funky fabric. Ask friends and family if they have old clothes, bed linen or curtains you could cut up and reuse.

Felt
Fabric shops, department stores, craft shops and toy shops often have felt.

Glue
Stationery shops and toyshops sell PVA glue and paper glue.

Needles
From sewing shops. Look for a variety pack with lots of different sizes.

Old clothes
As well as reusing your own old fabrics, ask family members for anything they don't want any more, and check out charity shops and jumble sales.

Online
There are many fabric and craft shops on the Internet. You may find the following sites useful starting points:
www.handyhippo.co.uk
www.hobbycraft.co.uk
www.myfabrics.co.uk

Paint, felt tips and paintbrushes
A toyshop is best for these, if you don't have them around at home.

Pins
From sewing shops. Longer pins with ball-shaped heads are the easiest to use.

Ribbons
Sewing and fabric shops usually sell ribbons and trimmings by the metre.

Scissors
The sharper your scissors, the easier they are to work with, but take care when using them.

Sequins
You can often find these at craft shops and stationer's.

Sewing machines

This book doesn't show you how to use a sewing machine, but if you have one, you can use it for most of the projects. Follow the machine's instructions, and get an adult to help you. If you want to buy a sewing machine, try a department store or sewing shop.

Stencils

You can get ready-made wall stencils at DIY and craft shops.

Thread

From sewing shops. It's worth buying good quality thread as it's easier to sew with. Use extra-strong thread for sewing through heavy fabrics.

Glossary

acrylic paint
A type of hardwearing, quick-drying paint.

appliqué
A technique used to decorate clothing or other fabric items by attaching fabric shapes.

backstitch
A strong sewing stitch that goes over each part of the fabric twice.

bunting
Strings of colourful flags.

cushion inner
The inside part of a cushion.

decoupage
Covering something with glued-on paper scraps.

Earth's resources
Materials or energy from the Earth.

embroidery
Using coloured thread to decorate fabric.

fabric tape
Strong, ribbon-like tape made of woven fabric.

font
A style of lettering.

gather
To pull fabric together into a bundle or crinkle using a line of stitching.

hem
The edge of a piece of fabric, folded over and sewn in place to stop it unravelling.

landfill
A place where rubbish is buried in the ground.

overstitch
A looping sewing stitch for sewing along edges.

raw edge
The unfinished or cut edge of a piece of fabric.

remnants
Leftover pieces of fabric.

running stitch
A simple, in-and-out sewing stitch.

sequins
Little shiny or metallic discs with a hole in the middle.

sheer
Very thin, or partly see-through.

stencil
A cut-out shape for colouring or painting through.

Index